office
DARES

SADIE CAYMAN

summersdale

OFFICE DARES

First published in 2005
Reprinted 2008 and 2010
This edition copyright © Summerdale Publishers Ltd, 2016

Summersdale Publishers Ltd
46 West Street
Chichester
West Sussex
PO19 1RP
UK

www.summersdale.com

Printed and bound in Malta

ISBN: 978-1-84953-946-3

Substantial discounts on bulk quantities of Summersdale books are available to corporations, professional associations and other organisations. For details contact Nicky Douglas by telephone: +44 (0) 1243 756902, fax: +44 (0) 1243 786300 or email: nicky@summersdale.com

CONTENTS

ABOUT THE AUTHOR

Sadie Cayman works in a peaceful office in West Sussex and spends her time walking sideways to and from the photocopier. So far, she has never been sacked from a job. She is also the author of *Student Dares* and *Naughty Dares*.

INTRODUCTION

Do you feel the urge to spice things up a little? Are you are a nonconformist with a devilish sense of humour? Now is the time to embrace your inner delinquent. All that's required is this book (small enough to be hidden in any desk drawer), a strong head and an open mind.

Remember: we're all in this together, and it's up to each and every one of us to make the workplace a bit more tolerable.

DISCLAIMER

Playing *Office Dares* won't reward you with the promotion you've always dreamed of, but rest assured that you'll leave the office knowing that you've brightened up the day of every colleague. Or just confused the hell out of them.

A NOTE ON THE POINTS SYSTEM

The dares have been given a carefully graded point system. Warm yourself up with the 1-point dares: they're perfect for the confident beginner or your first day with a new company.

The 3-point dares are relatively easy to perform but are often so subtle they may go unnoticed.

The 5-point dares are not to be taken lightly. They're challenging and somewhat outrageous. Expect very puzzled glances and to lose friends.

If your contract is coming to an end, by all means turn straight to the 10-point dares. Don't blame me for the consequences.

Play the game, if you dare…

AT YOUR DESK

While hiding from your boss behind that stack of papers, there's a lot of fun to be had using your phone, your workspace and your imagination.

DARE 1

Leave a message for a colleague that Mike Rotch or I. P. Freely called. Give a fake number, sit back and enjoy listening to them returning the call.

Rating: ⭐

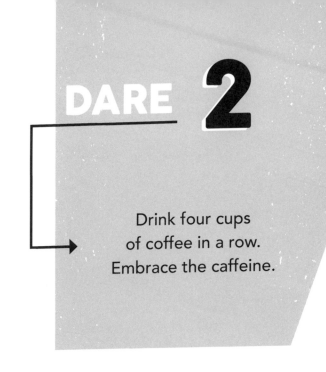

DARE 2

Drink four cups
of coffee in a row.
Embrace the caffeine.

Rating: ⭐

DARE 3

Vacuum around
your desk –
for half an hour.
If anybody complains,
chase them with
the hoover.

Rating:

DARE 4

Drop your chair as low as it will go. Complain loudly that your desk is too high.

Rating: ★

Change your company's
phone hold music
to death metal.

DARE 5

Rating: ⭐

DARE 6

Phone someone in the office you barely know, tell them who you are and declare, 'I just called to say I can't talk right now. Bye.'

Rating:

Keep a fork on your desk so that when your boss asks you to do something, you can look at them through the prongs and imagine them in jail.

DARE 7

Rating:

Leave a note marked *URGENT* on a colleague's desk, saying, *I need those figures by lunchtime. This deadline CANNOT be extended.* Leave no contact details.

DARE 8

Rating: ⭐

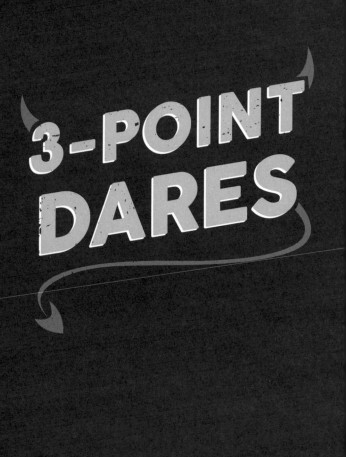

DARE 1

Ask a colleague to explain something very complicated. Interrupt them midway by saying, 'I'm sorry, I don't have time for this. Some of us have got work to do.'

Rating:

DARE 2

Mumble incoherently to a colleague and then say, 'I hope you got that – I don't want to have to repeat myself.'

Rating: ★ ★ ★

DARE

Create a photo collage of your 'pets' to pin above your desk. The more obscure the better, e.g. a blue whale, a condor and a northern hairy-nosed wombat.

Rating: ⭐ ⭐ ⭐

DARE 4

Bring a framed photograph of the royal family to work and mount it on the wall. Tell people it inspires you. Bow or curtsy to it at intervals throughout the day.

Rating: ★ ★ ★

Sit on your chair in the lotus position for 20 minutes. If anyone tries to talk to you, look them in the eye and put your finger on your lips.

DARE **5**

Rating:

DARE 6

Hang mosquito netting around your workspace and play tropical rainforest music all day.

Rating:

Start the day by recalling
a Neil Diamond quote.
Add it to your email
signature and refer
to it in meetings
whenever possible.

DARE 7

Rating: ★ ★ ★

Bring in a guitar or ukulele and hold an impromptu singalong during your tea break. Award yourself an extra point if you can get more than four colleagues to sing along with you.

DARE 8

Rating: ★ ★ ★

DARE

Start each working day by standing on your chair and reading aloud your favourite poem. Give yourself a round of applause at the end.

Rating:

DARE 1

Practise yoga at your desk for an hour at lunchtime. Award yourself an extra point for playing soothing music during your workout.

Rating:

DARE 2

Decorate your workspace with pictures of Ant and Dec. Try to pass them off as your brothers.

Rating: ★ ★ ★ ★ ★

DARE 3

Cover the lenses of your glasses with pictures of eyes cut out of magazines. Put them on every time your boss passes your desk.

Rating:

DARE 4

Wear sport gear to work,
e.g. cricket whites,
a scuba mask
or boxing gloves.
Tell people you're
'in training'.

Rating: ★ ★ ★ ★ ★

Build a fort around your desk using old cardboard boxes. Tell people they need to ask your permission to enter.

DARE **5**

Rating: ★ ★ ★ ★ ★

DARE

Fashion a long poking
device out of office
stationery. Use it to stroke
your colleague's face while
they're on the phone.

Rating: ★ ★ ★ ★ ★

Clamp your hands over your head to signal the end of a conversation, whether your colleague has finished talking or not.

DARE **7**

Rating: ★ ★ ★ ★ ★

10-POINT DARES

DARE 1

Write an elaborate resignation letter, detailing your boss's shortcomings and personal hygiene problems. Add a PTO note, *Only kidding.*

Rating:

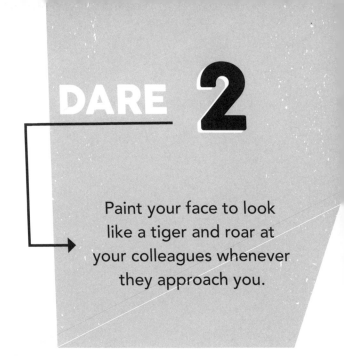

DARE 2

Paint your face to look like a tiger and roar at your colleagues whenever they approach you.

Rating: ★ ★ ★ ★ ★ ★ ★ ★ ★ ★

SCORES

There were total of **92** points up for grabs in this section.

If you scored **0–20** points: Call yourself daring? You need to raise your game to be in with a chance of being crowned king or queen of the office.

If you scored **21–50** points: A good effort. Now move onto the meeting room dares: they will really test your skill.

If you scored **51+** points: Well done! That's the spirit.

IN A MEETING

You'll find that there are far more daring things to be getting up to than taking notes, nodding your head and pretending to listen.

DARE

Demand that your
colleagues address you
by your birth name,
Hugh Janus or
Lacie Bigshortz.

Rating: ⭐

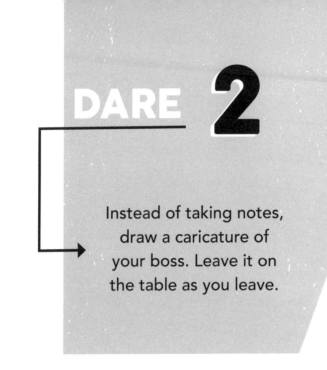

DARE 2

Instead of taking notes, draw a caricature of your boss. Leave it on the table as you leave.

Rating: ⭐

DARE 3

Spill coffee on the
conference table.
Make an origami boat
and sail it over the table.

Rating: ★

DARE 4

Finish every sentence
with the word 'dude',
e.g. 'The files are on
your desk, dude'.

Rating: ★

Stand up and demand
to know the real
reason the meeting
has been called.

DARE **5**

Rating: ⭐

DARE 6

Bring home-made
biscuits. As people start
to help themselves,
announce that you're
struggling with
constipation and
the main ingredient
is a laxative.

Rating: ⭐

Five days in advance of the next meeting, call each of your colleagues to tell them that you're unable to attend as you're not in the mood.

DARE **7**

Rating:

Refer to all of your colleagues as 'Frank'. If anyone asks why, say it's just easier to remember the name Frank.

DARE 8

Rating: ⭐

3-POINT DARES

DARE 1

While giving a presentation, button up your shirt one button out of sync. If anyone points it out, you reply, 'I know. I really prefer it this way.'

Rating:

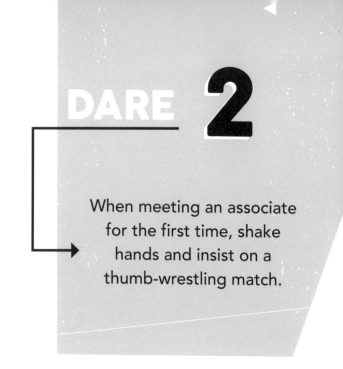

DARE 2

When meeting an associate
for the first time, shake
hands and insist on a
thumb-wrestling match.

Rating: ★ ★ ★

DARE 3

Slowly edge your chair towards the door over the course of the meeting. Swivel your chair as you do so.

Rating: ⭐ ⭐ ⭐

DARE 4

Pick a colleague.
Narrow your eyes
suspiciously at them
throughout the day.

Rating: ★ ★ ★

Kneel in front of the water cooler and drink directly from the nozzle.

DARE 5

Rating:

Say to your boss,
'I like your style'
and shoot them with
double-barrelled fingers.

Rating: ⭐ ⭐ ⭐

At the end of a meeting, drop a pen. When someone bends down to pick it up, scream, 'That's mine!' and run away. Later in the day, email them asking them not to touch your belongings in future.

DARE 7

Rating:

5-POINT
DARES

DARE 1

Arrive late, apologise and claim that you didn't have time for lunch so you'll be nibbling during the meeting. Eat an entire bag of raw carrots.

Rating:

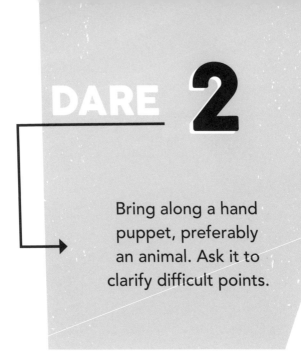

DARE 2

Bring along a hand puppet, preferably an animal. Ask it to clarify difficult points.

Rating: ★ ★ ★ ★ ★

DARE 3

At the end of the meeting, suggest that, for once, it would be nice if you concluded with the national anthem. Award yourself an extra point if you launch into it yourself.

Rating:

DARE 4

Present each of your colleagues with a cup of coffee and a biscuit. Smash each biscuit with your fist.

Rating: ★ ★ ★ ★ ★

Arrange toy figures on the table to represent each meeting attendee. Move them according to the movements of their real-life counterparts.

DARE **5**

Rating: ★ ★ ★ ★ ★

DARE 6

Pick an accent
different to your own.
Use it throughout
the entire meeting.

Rating: ★ ★ ★ ★ ★

Excuse yourself to
go to the bathroom.
Come back saying,
'Ah, I really needed that,'
and sigh with contentment.

DARE 7

Rating: ★ ★ ★ ★ ★

At a crucial moment, slap your forehead and mutter, 'Shut up, damn it. All of you, just shut up!'

DARE 8

Rating: ★★★★★

DARE 1

When addressing your colleagues, mispronounce their names, e.g. Rob Smith becomes Pob Sniff, Carol Baker becomes Barrel Maker and Sam Bailey becomes Ram Daily.

Rating: ★★★★★★★★★★★

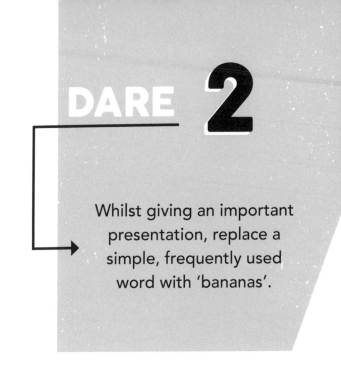

DARE 2

Whilst giving an important presentation, replace a simple, frequently used word with 'bananas'.

Rating: ★★★★★★★★★★

SCORES

There were a total of **89** points up for grabs in this section.

If you scored **0–20** points: Come on, loser, you can do better than that.

If you scored **21–50** points: You're really getting the hang of this now – and you're starting to love it, aren't you?

If you scored **51+** points: Excellent work. Have you noticed your boss's worry lines getting deeper?

AT YOUR COMPUTER

How did we all cope before the days of the internet and emails? Don't worry – you don't need to be a techno wizard to undertake these dares. All you need is a computer and a lot of courage.

DARE 1

On arrival at your desk, tell your computer that you don't want to fight today and that you're just doing your best.

Rating:

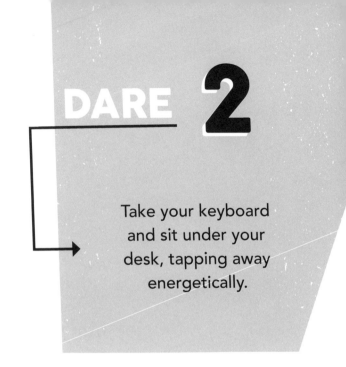

DARE 2

Take your keyboard
and sit under your
desk, tapping away
energetically.

Rating: ⭐

DARE

Set up a new out-of-office reply before your next day off, e.g. *Thank you for your message, which has been added to a queuing system. You are currently in 352nd place and you can expect a reply in Julember.*

Rating:

DARE 4

Put a chair in front of
the printer. Sit there
for an hour and explain
to passers-by that
you're waiting for an
important document.

Rating: ★

Set the ringtone of a
colleague's phone to
a sheep's baaing.

DARE 5

Rating: ★

DARE **6**

Frequently email the whole department with trivial information on your whereabouts, e.g. *My office will be closed at 3.42 p.m. for six minutes while I shred some important documents. Apologies for the inconvenience.*

Rating:

DARE 1

Cover a colleague's computer
screen with black paper. When
they have problems turning it
on, tell them that your computer
has been having issues too.
Award yourself an extra point
if they call a help desk.

Rating: ★ ★ ★

DARE 2

While you're waiting for documents to print, spin on your chair at high speed and sing the 'Hokey Cokey'.

Rating: ★ ★ ★

DARE 3

Send a company-wide email saying that there are cakes for everyone in the kitchen. When people complain that there weren't any, lean back, pat your stomach and say, 'Oh, you've got to be faster than that.'

Rating:

DARE 4

Speed up your boss's mouse so it's uncontrollable. If they comment on it, advise them to cut back on the caffeine.

Rating: ★ ★ ★

Wear rubber gloves whenever you use your computer. If your antics are questioned, repeatedly mutter, 'Infections... everywhere.'

DARE 5

Rating: ⭐ ⭐ ⭐

DARE 1

Tamper with your colleague's autocorrect on their email. Set it so that their name is autocorrected to *Ms/Mr Worky McWorkface*, or *'Hi all'* is changed to *'Greetings underlings'*.

Rating: ★★★★★

DARE 2

Set the screen saver of a colleague's computer to a slide show of unlikely heart-throbs, e.g. David Hasselhoff, Chesney Hawkes and Pat Sharp.

Rating: ★★★★★

DARE

Change your email address to the_wolf_man@companyname.com or lightning_bolt@companyname.com.

Rating:

DARE 4

Replace a colleague's mouse with some cheese and a note saying, *If you don't pay up, your mouse gets it.*

Rating:  ★ ★ ★ ★ ★

While a colleague leaves their desk unattended, change their email alert sound – the wackier the better. For an extra point, maximize the volume on their computer.

DARE

Rating: ★★★★★

DARE 1

Create a new company
letterhead and email
signature featuring a
picture of your favourite
superhero. Use these to
send out all your boss's
correspondence for a week.

Rating: ★★★★★★★★★★

DARE 2

Type up a detailed email to a 'personal friend' about an STI that you've caught. Mention that you believe the infection to be highly contagious. 'Accidentally' send the email to everyone in the office.

Rating:

SCORES

There were a total of **67** points up for grabs in this section.

If you scored **0–25** points: Why are you wasting your time?

If you scored **26–45** points: Great work. Well done.

If you scored **46+** points: You're a shining example of daring behaviour. Bravo!

OFFICE ETIQUETTE

The office is a strange place. Often an eclectic mix of people from all backgrounds and of different ages can be found in one building. This, to me, sounds like the perfect location for some interesting dares.

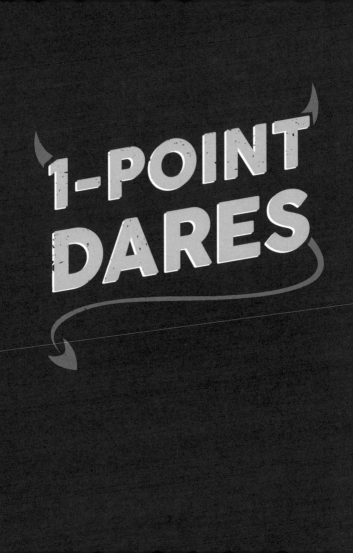

DARE 1

Attach a sign to the printer that says, *This printer is now installed with voice-recognition software. Instructions: stand closely and speak commands to printer, e.g. 'print' or 'scan'. You may need to repeat commands as printer is still in training mode.*

Rating:

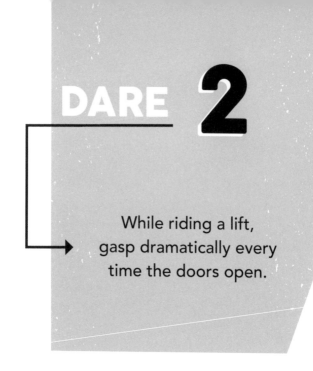

DARE 2

While riding a lift,
gasp dramatically every
time the doors open.

Rating: ⭐

DARE 3

Call your colleagues
'Champ' and 'Tiger'.
Encourage the others to call
you 'Coach'. Make sure to
high five your colleagues
at every opportunity.

Rating: ★

DARE

Walk sideways to the photocopier. If anybody stares at you, look worried and speed up.

Rating: ⭐

Ignore the first five people who say good morning to you. Kiss the sixth.

DARE **5**

Rating:

DARE 6

No matter what
anyone asks you,
reply 'Yes'.
Keep this up for
an entire day.

Rating:

Stick a terrifyingly bad
photo of a colleague
to the inner lid of
the photocopier.

DARE

Rating: ⭐

Announce when you're
going to the bathroom.
Be sure to specify which
number it will be.

DARE 8

Rating:

DARE 1

Run a lap of the office at high speed. Gain an extra point for every member of staff you manage to persuade to compete against you.

Rating:

DARE 2

Arrive at work wearing combats and a balaclava. When questioned, reply, 'I'm afraid I can't talk about it.'

Rating: ★ ★ ★

DARE 3

Hang a long piece of
toilet roll from the
back of your outfit. Act
genuinely surprised when
someone points it out.

Rating: ★ ★ ★

Improvise rap lyrics about everyone you encounter at work.

Rating:

Put up a chart in the toilet
so that staff can keep
notes about their poos
(time, size, colour, etc.).

DARE **5**

Rating: ⭐ ⭐ ⭐

DARE 6

Leave a mug
face down in the
kitchen with a note that
says, *Only move this
mug if you're able to
kill what's underneath.*

Rating:  ★ ★ ★

Go into the fridge and leave notes on everybody else's food but your own, saying, *Not Debbie's*.

DARE **7**

Rating: ★ ★ ★

Make up nicknames for all your colleagues and only refer to them by these names, e.g. 'No, I'm sorry. I'm going to have to disagree with you there, Chachi.'

DARE 8

Rating: ★ ★ ★

5-POINT DARES

DARE 1

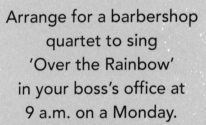

Arrange for a barbershop
quartet to sing
'Over the Rainbow'
in your boss's office at
9 a.m. on a Monday.

Rating:  ★ ★ ★ ★ ★

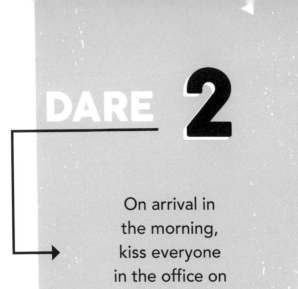

DARE 2

On arrival in
the morning,
kiss everyone
in the office on
both cheeks.

Rating: ★ ★ ★ ★ ★

DARE

When you first encounter your boss in the morning, give him or her a hug and say, in clear earshot of your colleagues, 'Don't worry, we'll get through this together.'

Rating:

If someone offers to
make you a cup of tea,
break into uncontrollable
sobs and exclaim,
'That is the nicest thing
anyone has ever said
to me.' Ask for a hug.

Rating: ★ ★ ★ ★ ★

Walk into your boss's office
and have this conversation:
You: 'Can you hear that?'
Your boss: 'What?'
You: 'Never mind,
it's gone now.'
Repeat at regular intervals
throughout the day.

DARE **5**

Rating:

DARE 6

Walk into a very busy person's office and, while they watch you with growing irritation, turn the light switch off and on ten times.

Rating: ★ ★ ★ ★ ★

Eat five doughnuts at lunch without licking your lips. If someone points out the sugar on your face, look puzzled and tell them it's your beard. Extra point for a female contender.

DARE 5

Rating:

Make yourself a handy office utility belt and fill it with your stationery. Have a stapler in each pocket and wield them like weapons at passing colleagues.

DARE 8

Rating: ★ ★ ★ ★ ★

DARE 1

Feign a crush on a doll or teddy and carry it around the office. Take it to lunch in the canteen, insist on giving it its own chair... You get the idea.

Rating: ★★★★★★★★★★★★

DARE 2

Point at your boss and accuse him/her of farting and stinking out the entire office. Bonus point for walking out of the room appalled.

Rating: ★ ★ ★ ★ ★ ★ ★ ★ ★ ★

SCORES

There were a total of **65** points up for grabs in this section.

If you scored **0–20** points: Give this book to someone with balls.

If you scored **21–40** points: Good work. Give yourself a pat on the back.

If you scored **41+** points: Wow. I'm in awe of you.

YOUR GRAND TOTAL

There were a total of **313** points up for grabs in this book.

If you scored **0–125** points: You're a loser – simple as that. You deserve every moment of office boredom coming to you.

If you scored **126–250** points: Well, you certainly tried, didn't you? You deserve a medal for all the stupid things you've done and for all the confusion you've inflicted upon your colleagues.

If you scored **251+** points: You're the ultimate daredevil, on a par with Evel Knievel. You're officially king/queen of the office.

If you're interested in finding out more about our books, find us on Facebook at **Summersdale Publishers** and follow us on Twitter at **@Summersdale**.

www.summersdale.com